My Country
India

Jillian Powell

W
FRANKLIN WATTS

This edition 2013

First published in 2012
by Franklin Watts

Copyright © Franklin Watts 2012

Franklin Watts
338 Euston Road
London NW1 3BH

Franklin Watts Australia
Level 17/207 Kent Street
Sydney, NSW 2000

All rights reserved.

Dewey number: 954'.0532
PB ISBN: 978 1 4451 2700 2
Library eBook ISBN: 978 1 4451 2433 9

Printed in Malaysia

Series Editor: Paul Rockett
Series Designer: Paul Cherrill
 for Basement68
Picture Researcher: Diana Morris

Franklin Watts is a division of
Hachette Children's Books,
an Hachette UK company.

www.hachette.co.uk

Every attempt has been made to clear copyright.
Should there be any inadvertent omission please apply
to the publisher for rectification.

Picture credits: Neale Cousland/Shutterstock: 3, 20; Dario
Diment/Shutterstock: 11t; Nikhil Gangavane/Dreamstime: 19c;
Gavan Goulder/Alamy: 10; Mathes/Dreamstime: 16; Holger
Mette/istockphoto: front cover l; Erick N/Shutterstock: 8, 24;
neelsky/Shutterstock: 7, 21; Mikhail Nekrasov/Shutterstock: 11b;
nrg123/Shutterstock: front cover r; David Pearson/Alamy: 13;
Pawel Pietraszewski/Shutterstock: 5; Photos India Alamy: 14;
pixcub/Shutterstock: front cover c, 4t, 12b, 17b, 19b, 22t.; Paul
Prescott/Shutterstock: 15; Vikram Raghuvanshi/istockphoto: 1, 6;
Samrat35/Dreamstime: 17c, 18; Rikard Stadler/Shutterstock: 12t;
Przemyslaw Szablowski/Shutterstock: 22c; Alfonso de Thomas/
Shutterstock: 4b; Aleksandar Todorovic/Shutterstock: 2, 9.

Contents

India in the world   4

People who live in India   6

India's landscape   8

The weather in India   10

At home with my family   12

What we eat   14

Going to school   16

Festivals and celebrations   18

Things to see   20

Fast facts about India   22

Glossary and further information   23

Index   24

All words in **bold**
appear in the
glossary on page 23.

India in the world

My name is Ajita and I come from India.

I live in Mumbai, which is the largest city in India.

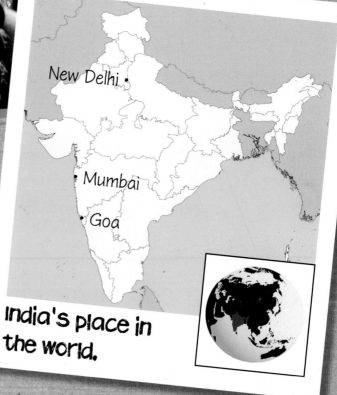

New Delhi

Mumbai

Goa

India's place in the world.

Mumbai is a busy city with lots of outdoor markets.

India is in South Asia. It has a long coastline and shares borders with countries including China, Nepal and Pakistan.

People who live in India

India has 400 million children, more than any other country.

More than a billion people live in India.

Many live in big, crowded cities, others in small villages in the countryside.

Most people speak Hindi and English, but there are over 400 local languages too.

Indians follow many different religions, including the Hindu, Muslim, Sikh and Christian faiths.

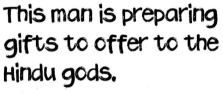

This man is preparing gifts to offer to the Hindu gods.

India's landscape

India has many different kinds of landscape, from mountains and **deserts** to **plains** and **tropical** jungles.

Camels are used to carry people and goods across the deserts in northern India.

Almost half of India is used for farming animals and growing crops, such as rice, wheat and tea.

In the north are the Himalayas, the highest mountain range in the world.

This woman is picking tea leaves. Tea from India is sold all over the world.

 # The weather in India

Heavy monsoon rain often causes floods. This man's rickshaw is caught in them.

India has three seasons — one is hot, one is wet and one is cool.

The wet or **monsoon** season starts in the south in early June and moves north by July.

The northern highlands have a cooler climate than the south, where it is mostly very **humid**.

In the north, the tops of the Himalayan mountains are always covered in snow.

Goa, in the south, has long, sandy beaches which make it popular with tourists.

At home with my family

Most flats have balconies where people can hang their washing to dry.

I live with my mother and father and my sister in a flat in Mumbai.

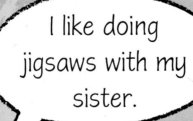

I like doing jigsaws with my sister.

I share a room with my sister. At home we like playing games and drawing together.

Sometimes we go shopping to one of the big malls, then we go to the cinema.

The film industry in India is the largest in the world. Three billion people go to the cinema each year.

What we eat

At breakfast we have toast and fruit and drink tea or fruit juice. Mum packs me a hot lunch for school in small tins called dabbas.

These dabbas contain rice and curry.

In the evening we all sit down for a meal together. We like eating **spicy** vegetable dishes with rice and also sweet milk and rice puddings.

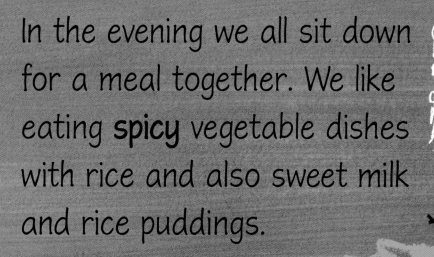
Mum buys vegetables from the market. Like many Hindu families, we don't eat meat.

Going to school

We start primary school when we are five or six. My sister and I catch the bus to school each day.

Some of my friends take an autorickshaw to school.

We always start the day with prayers in assembly.

Then we have lessons in English and Hindi, maths, science and art.

Festivals and celebrations

There are lots of colourful festivals in India all through the year. Holi is the spring festival of colours.

To celebrate Holi, people cover each other in powder paints.

Diwali is the autumn festival of lights. We decorate our homes with lights and candles and have firework displays.

People also get together to enjoy street carnivals and harvest celebrations.

For Diwali, people draw patterns in coloured chalk or powder outside their homes.

I like Diwali because we have sweets and fireworks!

Things to see

Many people who come to India visit the Taj Mahal, which was built in memory of an Indian emperor's queen.

Over three million people visit the Taj Mahal each year!

Visiting the National Parks to see tigers and elephants is very popular.

India has the largest number of tigers living in the wild.

Here are some facts about my country!

Fast facts about India

Capital city = New Delhi

Population = 1.2 billion

Area = 1.2 million km^2

Main languages = Hindi, English and 16 other official languages

National holiday = Independence Day

Currency = Rupee

Main religions = Hinduism, Islam, Christianity, Sikhism, Buddhism, Jainism

Longest river = the Ganges (2,525km)

Highest mountain = Kanchenjunga in the Himalayas (8,586m)

Glossary

dabbas small tins or tiffin boxes that stack together

deserts areas of land which get little or no rain

humid damp

monsoon seasonal rains

plains flat areas of land mostly without trees

rickshaw a small two- or three-wheeled vehicle, hand-pulled
 or motorised

spicy food cooked with spices

tropical belonging to hot countries close to the Earth's equator

Websites

www.activityvillage.co.uk/india_for_kids.htm
Printable fact sheets, worksheets and craft activities about India.

www.bbc.co.uk/learningzone/clips/life-in-mumbai-pt-3-3/5912.html
A video showing family life in Mumbai.

http://india.gov.in/knowindia/kids.php
The children's section of the Indian government's website, including facts
on the Indian currency, flag, culture and history.

Books

Been There: India by Annabel Savery (Franklin Watts, 2011)

The Big Picture: Market by Catherine Chambers
(A & C Black Publishers Ltd, 2011)

Countries: India by Ruth Thomson (Wayland, 2010)

Index

beaches 11

celebrations 18–19
cinema 13
coastline 5

deserts 8
Diwali 19

family life 12–13
farming 9
festivals 18–19
flag 22
food 14–15

Goa 4, 11

Himalayas 9, 11, 22
Hinduism 7, 15, 22
Holi 18

landscape 8–9
languages 7, 22

monsoon 10
mountains 8, 9, 11, 22
Mumbai 4, 5, 12

National Parks 21

people 6–7
population 6, 22

religion 7, 15, 22

school 14, 16–17

Taj Mahal 20
tea 9
tourism 11, 20–21

weather 10–11